HELP SAVE AMERICA

JON LEWIS

outskirts
press

Table of Contents

Preface

We live in the best country in the world. Yet there are numerous people who are trying to destroy us. Just like Hitler in Germany, they are trying to remove our history and get us to hate each other. So far we have not had the problem of killing those who disagree with us. But will it last? It is up to us to save our great country.

Founding fathers

07/25/21

Before America became a country, there were many people who came here mostly from England and other European countries. They lived their own lives the way they wanted. They helped each other in so many ways.

As the county grew the King of England began forcing the Americans to live differently. The king started telling them how to live and imposed taxes on them. They had nothing to say about how their taxes were being spent. They no longer could live the way they wanted to live.

Soon the king sent soldiers here to make sure we lived like the king wanted us to live. This caused much discomfort among our citizens. They finally had enough and started a revolt. It became the revolutionary war so we could live our own lives.

Inequality

Inequality is a part of nature. If there is a pack of lions, there is only one leader. The rest of the pack follows the leader. It is the same for a flock of birds.

In school each student is given a grade. Why is it that some get an A while others get a B or C or F? They have the same teacher in the same classroom. In sports why is it that some excel while others just get by or are removed from the team?

How about work? If a person becomes a plumber, why is it that they end up becoming the owner of their own business? Or why is it that they never make more than the starting wage? Should they consider that they chose the wrong profession?

Acceptance to Preference

07/25/21

There has been so much discussion about racism lately. It used not be that way. However, if you disagree with some folks, you are called a racist. It doesn't matter if you are racist or not. If you are a Republican you must be racist according to the democrats or most of the media.

I am not racist and I know of nobody who is. When living in the DFW area, I had several black friends and business associates. When I had my own business, one of my key managers was black and female.

According to the latest figures I can find, there are 6 white people for every black person. I watch a lot of TV. Lately, the advertisements are out of step with these numbers. Every ad has to have at least one black person. It doesn't matter if there is only one person in the ad or more. Some ads are all black.

My local stations come from the DFW

area. I get up early each day. I spend a lot of time outdoors. Hence, I watch the weather reports each chance I get. On weekdays, the people on the news are pretty much like real life. On weekends the early news comes on first on the NBC channel at 5:30. I watch it every day on the weekends. There are no white folks on this news. Racist whites? I doubt it!

Rather than being accepted they are being preferred. This is done by most of the media and by many companies. It is a way of dividing us. No longer can we be individuals and living life as we see fit, and helping others. Rather than being judged by what we do, we are judged by the color of our skin.

This is one part of those who hate America and want to destroy us. Having grown up in this great country, I can't understand it. They say America is a racist country. They ignore the fact that we have black chiefs of police, mayors, representatives, senators, and even a black president. It will be changed in time as voting comes. Most people agree with me. Let's get rid of the people who hate America.

Gun Violence

07/25/21

With all the gun violence taking place in major cities in our country, too many people are blaming the problem on guns. Too many want to ban the ownership of guns. They blame assault rifles on the problem. Also, they blame gun dealers. They forget that we already have laws in place to regulate gun dealers. Of course these are for legal gun dealers. Those who sell guns illegally don't care about the laws.

I have owned guns for over 50 years. These are both rifles and pistols. They remain in my closet. None have ever shot another person. They have shot numerous animals but not people.

If there were ever a true investigation into those who have shot other people, I suspect they will find some new information. I doubt that any of them have been to vacation bible school, or Sunday school, or church. I seriously doubt that any have seen the inside of a church.

They are criminals, period. They should be in jail and not on our streets. Too many major cities don't ever put them in jail. If so, they are released shortly afterwards. Very few if any are prosecuted. They are put back on the streets to shoot somebody else. How does this solve anything?

Climate change

"Those who forget about history are doomed to repeat it" I forgot who first said that but it remains true today as when it was first said. You can relate to this as you continue reading.

It was first called "Man Made Global Warming." The history of climate temperature was demonstrated by the curve referred to as the "Hockey Stick". It showed that the global temperature was increased dramatically as man began to add energy to the world. This alarmed the scientists of bad things to happen in the future. As time passed and others began to investigate, it was found that the scientists that developed the Hockey Stick curve manufactured the data so they could get grants to improve their income. This was not published except by a small bunch interested in the truth.

In the 1970's, before the internet, Life Magazine was one of the most respected magazines and sources of information in America. One of their publications was "The Coming

Ice Age". This was written and supported by scientists. Big change happened when Hockey Stick curve was invented.

There has been much discussion about the melting ice near the north pole. When in high school we once studied the Northwest Passage. Didn't spend a lot of time on it but it was mentioned. Essentially it is how sailboats, before ice breakers, sailed from the Atlantic Ocean to the Pacific Ocean between Canada and the North Pole. Somehow the ice had melted before our today's alert. How could that be?

In 2021 the northwest part of America was experiencing record high temperatures. At almost the same time in Texas they were experiencing record low temperatures. How could this happen?

Green new deal

This is a government program to deal with the myth of manmade Climate Change. It is supported by many politicians who have no science background and rarely look for facts about their proposals. Many bring doubt about their intelligence when they speak and write. It is designed to provide us with electric power without petroleum products.

Texas is the leading state for wind power. It also has very many solar panels. In February 2021, Texas suffered many blackouts and too many people were without electric power for days. When the weather had temperatures reach new record lows, it snowed almost to record levels. The wind stopped blowing and the sun was blocked by all the snow clouds. This could happen again in Texas and other states. People couldn't charge their phones or computers. Thus, it affected communications. With the record lows and no electric power, many homes had water pipes break and flood their homes.

Now Texas is working on restarting petroleum powered stations. Where they were shut down before, they are being restated to restore power. They will be able to shut down and restart in case of another power problem. They won't be running all the time since the wind and sun will provide power.

Our intelligent (?) government shut down one of our pipe lines. Where we were an exporter of petroleum products, that is now no longer the case. Another pipe line was hacked. It lead to gas shortages along the east coast of America. It has been restored but was a real problem.

Since shutting down our pipe line, we have helped restart a pipe line from Russia to Germany. I'm sorry but I can't understand why we support Russia and punish America. Where we were an exporter of petroleum products, we are back to being and importer from countries that hate us.

Electric cars

07/25/21

There is lots of excitement about electric cars these days. It appears that they are the future of transportation. Only good things are mentioned about them. I remain unconvinced.

Electric cars are very expensive. You can almost buy two regular cars for the price of one electric car. That rules out many potential buyers but they are selling quite well these days. It would be even worse if not for the government subsidies.

Using an electric car means you don't have to spend your money on gas. How much will that save you for the life of the car? I have some questions. Is the charger included in the purchase price or do you have to pay more to be able to charge your car at home? Also, is the electricity to charge the car free? I doubt it. Your gas bill may go down but your electric bill will go up? By how much is not disclosed. I recently saw a paper where the miles per gallon is less that 10 considering the cost of electricity.

The latest is a new electric car that goes from 0 to 60 in 2 seconds. I find that unbelievable. If the wheels can turn fast enough to achieve this speed, the car will not move as the wheels spin in place.

One of the biggest costs of electric cars is the batteries. They don't last forever. I can't find any information on how long they last nor the cost of replacement. I have some battery powered tools for my yard work. They work great but the replacement cost of new batteries is almost as much as buying a new tool. I can't tell how much effect they have on my electric bill each month. Since I don't use them every day it is almost impossible to tell how much electric power it takes to keep them charged.

This is another case where government interference is distorting reality. How many people would buy an electric car if the government did not pay subsidies to the manufacturer to reduce the purchase price? I dislike my taxes being raised to reduce the purchase price of an electric car. I think the electric car should compete against regular cars on their own.

Education

07/21/21

Education should begin in childhood. When I was in school, every class had an American flag in the room. We started each day with the pledge of allegiance. This was followed by a prayer over the intercom. We did not know it at the time but we lived in the greatest county known to man.

When growing up I attended the Baptist church. Each Sunday I attended Sunday School Class. I learned at an early age how to treat others in life. When I was married, I attended Methodist church. My kids learned how to treat others at an early age. When I lived at Hideaway Lake, I attended the church there which was non-denominational but with a Baptist flavor. Now that I live in the country on the family place, I rarely attend church. However, my early learning allows me to live a more Christian life than most of those who are in church every time the doors open.

I have an advanced degree in physics. However, most of what I have used in my life has been learned outside of traditional education. The library is a good source of education. So are the various sources outside traditional education. I learned a lot from books like Excel for Dummies and other similar books. It took some work but was well worth it.

Today, so many young folks are focusing on a 4-year degree. They major in obscure areas that have no use in business and can't get a decent job after graduation. Unfortunately, too many take out loans to pay for their degree and are in debt for many years after graduation. I worked my way through college and so did my kids. Graduation without debt but took more than 4 years. Well worth it.

An alternative to traditional degrees, are technical schools. It is typically, only a 2 year program. You graduate with skills to go to work at a fair pay scale. There are also CDL schools where you can become a truck driver. It has great pay but with unusual working hours and days. School is not long term.

A story I like to tell is about a person with a great job and great pay moves into a house at the end of a cul-de-sac. After getting in and settled somewhat, he noticed his next door neighbor was in a huge house with several very high priced cars in the driveway. He went to introduce himself. He asked the neighbor what kind of job he had. The neighbor told him that before becoming a plumber he was a brain surgeon. It's not what school you go to it is what you do afterwards.

Political parties

07/21/21

Today we have the Republican party, the Democrat party, and other less active parties. I grew up in Texas. Back then the winner of the Democrat party primary would become the winner of the election. Today things are not that way. There are almost as many Democrats as Republicans.

There have been too many frauds in our elections. Dead people are allowed to vote. Obviously, they did not vote in person. We have absentee votes where the voter must request a ballot which is good for those who have problems getting to the pole to vote. They must sign the ballot and include proof of name to submit the absentee vote. There have also been vote gathering where some folks can get absentee voters election papers and alter them or fill them in to vote to remove good candidates.

Most of this fraud has been committed by Democrats. They have succeeded too many times. One of our great presidents was

Ronald Reagan. He was once a Democrat but changed to a Republican. He stated that he did not change, the party changed. This is verification that this change has been going on for some time and is not something new.

Having an open mind, I did attend the Republican meetings, the Tea Party meetings, and the Democrat meetings. The head of the local Democrat part was Mike Human. The two of us had a mutual respect relationship. We got along great. I enjoyed the Democrat meetings as well as the other meetings. I didn't agree with all aspects of the Democrat meetings but did respect the opinion of the other members. Mike Human passed away. Since then I have not been invited to any Democrat meetings.

This seems to be the way the "new" Democrats think. If you disagree with anything that they propose you are excluded. You may be called a racist or some other derogatory name. This may be the way for us to return to being Americans again. As they continue to try to degrade our country, they are upsetting some of the traditional members of the party. Those who have voted Democrat all their adult life are beginning to wonder what happened to their party.

Save the Democrat party

07/22/21

The Democrat party has been infiltrated by people who hate America. I can't understand why so many wealthy people support this party. Do they want their company to be owned by the government? I also don't understand why those people who always voted Democrat still do. Are they happy with some unknown person in government telling them how to live their life?

We hear such things on new laws such as "If you want to know what is in the bill, you have to pass it." A bill that may become law is written behind closed doors by who knows who. As bad as this sounds, it is worse by those who vote to pass the bill. Who are these people who blindly vote to have new laws that have the government telling them how to live their lives?

We have Democrat members of congress whose only qualifications are being a bar tender and a loud mouth. There are other Democrat members of congress that are Muslims who hate America and want to destroy it. What are the Democrat voters thinking? Do they want the government telling them how to live their lives?

What are the duties of our representatives and senators? It is to act in the best interest of their district or state. It is not to follow the leader. Too many follow the leader to perhaps gain additional income by being chosen to lead a group rather than act in favor of those who voted them into office.

Not all Republicans are good but most are. Not all Democrats are bad but most are. We need to remember that their duty is to make America a better place to live in freedom and allow us to live our life as we see fit and not by some unknown person in the capital.

In future elections, especially in the 2022 mid-term, Democrats must vote out the existing members or vote for the Republican candidate. This will make a big change in congress. It will be a major defeat for the Democrats. With the major defeat facing them, the Democrats will start to evaluate their position on so many aspects. Will they start to think about their positions on many fronts? I hope and think that they will make a major change in their philosophy. America will be saved.

Conclusion

07/26/21

We are so lucky in the area where I live. We have some great leaders who are making the changes needed to return Texas to a great state. We have Bryan Slaton as our state representative and Bob Hall as our state senator. We also have Dwayne Collins who is not an elected official but a great leader in helping return our state to where it should be.

In high school we had a course in American history. We also had a course in Texas history. Where America was freed from England to become a separate country, Texas was freed from Mexico to become a separate country. Texas later became a state in America.

In the early days, if a democrat was elected in the primary, he became the elected official in the state. Those who want to destroy our state began running in the Republican primaries. Too many of those were Republican in Name Only (RINO). We had speakers of the house appoint democrats as leaders of various committees. That may be changing. At least I hope so.

"United we stand, divided we fall" I forgot who said that but it is so true. Those who want to destroy our country are promoting the divided part. False claims of women being diminished and claims of racism are absolutely false. There is no relationship with reality. Just ways to hate each other.

The media and many large companies are not helping. They are supporting Democrats. They made their fortunes in our capitalist country. Do they really want their companies controlled by some idiot in Washington, DC? Will they be fired for no reason and replaced with another idiot?

Our education system is a big player in this possible destruction of our country. They are teaching our children and young adults to hate American. What would they say if the schools and colleges where controlled by idiots in Washington, DC? Perhaps they would be fired and replaced with others who are even worse.

It is up to us, individual voters, to make the changes. Lifelong Democrats need to evaluate if they are getting the results they desire. If Democrats are defeated at the polls, they will start to look at themselves. Will they make changes to survive or continue with defeat? Will they follow the way Texas was saved or continue to even greater defeats. Let's hope they make the right choices.

About The Author

The author lives about an hour east of Dallas, Texas. He grew up half way between Dallas and Fort Worth, Texas. He has witnessed how the direction of the politics in the state have been changing. From a Democrat controlled state to a Republican controlled state. He has also witnessed how the wrong people have been infiltrating the state politics. He has also witnessed how corrections are being made to return Texas to a great state much like the beginning of America.